Marguerite Cook

Primary Songs

Marguerite Cook

Primary Songs

ISBN/EAN: 9783337182076

Printed in Europe, USA, Canada, Australia, Japan

Cover: Foto ©Thomas Meinert / pixelio.de

More available books at **www.hansebooks.com**

PRIMARY

SONGS,

EDITED BY

MRS. D. C. COOK,

ASSISTED BY THE

BUREAU OF   AND   BUREAU OF

PRIMARY S. S. MUSIC.   **PRIMARY S.S. POETRY.**

MRS. D. A. GREENMAN.	ALICE W. KNOX.
T. MARTIN TOWNE.	MRS. C. H. PERRY.
WILL OGELBY.	MRS. J. W. BURDETTE.
W. S. B. MATHEWS.	MRS. M. A. MORSE.
J. M. STILLMAN.	T. MARTIN TOWNE.

PUBLISHED BY

DAVID C. COOK PUB. CO.,

36 Washington St.

CHICAGO, ILL.

PRIMARY MUSIC.

ITS OBJECT.

We often hear this remark: "There is no use trying to teach my class to sing. I don't believe children in the infant class understand what they sing. So what is the use of wasting their time?" We are happy to say that teachers of this opinion are scarce. Nevertheless, that some so reason, is a fact, for there are primary classes which never even try to sing. So it is perhaps well for us to inquire into the object of primary singing. Says one teacher: "We always sing while the papers and cards are being distributed, and the collection is being taken up, it drowns the noise beautifully." Says another: "We sing to use up the time. I always let them sing everything they know; then when the other work is done, there is only a few minutes left for the lesson, and that is just what I like, for I never know what to say to them."

How these teachers exalt music! They make me think of some remarks of T. Martin Towne in the Officers' Quarterly. Said he: "The singing in many of our schools, is simply the chinking, *the filling in* to the exercises. A pastor in Wisconsin once uttered the following: 'In order that the sexton may poke the fire, we will sing ' Nearer My God to Thee.'

"The essence of the remark is often extracted and instilled into the exercises of singing in some of our best schools. In order that the teachers may get their classes in order, that late pupils may straggle in, that the minister may take off his overcoat, we will sing! Now when this course is indulged in, how does music elevate the mind or the soul?"

If this were the sole object of singing in the primary class we should at once agree with our sisters, who say "There is no use in it." But such is not the use put to music in many schools. The little ones are taught to sing that their minds may the more readily grasp the truths of the gospel thus presented to them in a pleasing, attractive form. Their singing is also an expression of their praise to God. Appropriate little songs sung at intervals as they fit into the work of the session form a pleasant variety, thus accomplishing a double purpose as a means of worship, and at the same time a means of pleasant recreation.

This we believe to be the true object of singing in the primary class as well as in every other class. This being the object, all will agree that singing in the primary class is very desirable. The question then arises

WHAT SHALL WE SING?

Bright lively tunes with words so simple as to be understood by all the children should, if possible, be selected. It is painful to hear little children in the primary class struggling through some long solemn tune, the words of which are unintelligible to them. A song to be simple, need not necessarily be silly, the sentiment should be sense. Let the teaching be practical—something that the children can understand and appreciate. "He loves me too," conveys more to their minds than many a much more elaborate production would do. In regard to primary pieces, written in more than one part, let us say that the melody only is intended to be sung by the whole class. The other parts are intended to be used by the organist or pianist.

In regard to the pieces containing responses, our experience has been very pleasant—with a little drill a class will sing heartily and correctly every one of them. They even seem to enjoy them better than the other pieces on account of the variety which they afford. The responses, of course, should be simple and sung by a portion of the class. Let us sing, if possible, songs whose teachings bear upon the lessons of the day. For this purpose a lesson verse is found upon the "Illuminated Lessons" and "Dew Drops." The children receiving them have a chance to read the words, or better still, commit them to memory. They are also found in the "Primary Teacher" and "Primary Songs." So the teacher has them before her. As the tune is the same for a whole quarter it will be a very easy matter to sing at least one verse, each Sabbath, which has been written on the lesson.

The children should be taught a number of pieces. Do not depend upon one or two "old stand-bys;" teach them enough so that you are never at a loss for something new, for an old song is new to them if it has not been heard for two or three weeks.

It may at first seem difficult to teach many new songs; but in this, as in everything else, there is nothing like practice, each new one you learn will seem easier than the last. When the children once get into the way and spirit of learning and singing new songs there will be little difficulty.

HOW TO LEARN NEW SONGS.

It may at first seem impossible to teach new songs, but if you persist in the determination to teach *at least* one new song each month, and that each one shall be thoroughly learned before another is begun, you will gradually find the work becoming easier, and will find it a pleasant work.

Some teachers say, "I can teach the words, but I cannot sing. So I cannot teach the tune." To them I would say, select four or five of your best singers, play for them, or if you do not play yourself get some friend to play for them the melody, slowly at first until they catch it. They will sing an ordinary tune after hearing it played five or six times, and will sing it correctly, too. Let these form your little choir the next Sabbath, and with their help as leaders the tune may be easily taught to a large class, even though the teacher may not be able to sing one note.

The piano or organ is a great help, as it gives the music correctly. I know that some differ on this point, but I would rather trust to a fine toned piano, correctly played, than to any voice. They learn, by following the piano to sing exactly. Most pieces at least deserve to be sung as they are written, which few classes will do without the aid of some instrument.

The word edition of the "Primary Songs" if placed in the hands of the children will save the teacher a great deal of labor in teaching the words. Some will object to this because some of the children cannot read. To those I would say, they will learn them a great deal sooner with your help and the help of a third of the class than they would with your help alone. The clear, ready tones of each child who can read will be just so much inducement to the timid ones to join in, or to those who cannot read to listen, that they too may add their voices. They will not be left in the background. For this reason we hope the word edition will be a great aid to the teacher in this respect.

WHEN TO SING.

Singing is a very pleasant and appropriate way in which to begin the exercises of the session. It is a pleasant way also to close the session. Then sometimes some thought on the lesson suggests a verse of some well-known piece which it would be well to sing just as it fits in.

If your class is getting tired or restless, get them on their feet and have them sing heartily a verse or two of some lively song. Visiting a primary class one Sabbath I noticed the class were getting listless and finally disorderly. The teacher tried in every way to claim their attention in vain. She seemed almost in despair At last a bright idea seemed to strike her, for her face lighted up and she broke out into that happy little song, "God sees the little sparrows fall." The noisy little fellows at once caught the spirit, and they irresistibly joined in with her, and that noisy, lazy atmosphere was changed, brightened and freshened as by a thunder shower. The lazy little ones aroused themselves; the noisy ones forgot to be noisy. That teacher knew when to sing, and she did not degrade music either, for those little folks never sang with better spirit.

If your pupils come early the time might be very profitably spent in practicing new songs. Sometimes half an hour after school might be spent in the same way.

HOW TO SING.

With spirit and understanding. Have the words and tune thoroughly learned and then allow no drawling. We sometimes hear classes sing as if there were a ten pound weight at the end of each note which they were obliged to drag out of the way before they could reach the next.

Teach them to throw back their shoulders, open their mouths and sing so distinctly that each word may be understood by a person not acquainted with the piece. Teach them to sing in strong, hearty tones. Singing the scale in strong staccato tones a few times is an excellent practice for them. They should not be allowed to drawl; neither should they be allowed to sing in a jerky, hipty-hop style. In order to sing properly it is necessary that the children understand the meaning of the words and the sentiments which they teach. The meaning should be thoroughly understood. We would not then be startled by hearing an infant class singing about the " Wishy woshy wever." Who would ever imagine they were singing " We will walk and worship ever!" did they not know "Shall we gather at the river?" They should know what they are singing, and should be taught to sing it earnestly, devoutly and reverently. You will not then be shocked by hearing boys screaming at the top of their lungs, " Jesus died on Calvary," while they are throwing spit balls at the boys opposite, or are sticking pins in their neighbors.

PRIMARY CHOIR.

A little plan which often works to advantage, is to select, say, ten of your best singers and call them your choir. In learning new pieces let them take the lead. Sometimes let them sing the verse and the whole class the chorus, or occasionally vary this by calling upon them for a solo or duet. This little choir will be a great help to the teacher in teaching new songs. They might be drilled at the school either before or after the session, or during the week at the home of the teacher or one of the choir. Each member of this little choir at least should have a copy of the " Primary Songs" or " Word Edition of Primary Songs."

This choir will do good service at your little concerts or exhibitions. The lesson verses, if thoroughly learned and sung by the whole class or this choir, will furnish a very nice part of the programme in the " quarterly review" of the whole school. As each lesson is reviewed, let the primary class sing the verse on that lesson, the result will please all.

MARGUERITE COOK.

We feel under greatest obligation to the hundreds who have responded to our call, by writing both words and music, and to the Bureaus of Primary Sunday-school Poetry and Sunday-school Music, who have so kindly assisted in grading, selecting, and arranging pieces, and shall only hope that the book will meet with similar approval of the Sunday-schools of the land.

M. C.

PRIMARY SONGS.

No. 1. We Have a Good and Gentle Lord.

Rev. Rob't Kerr.

T. Martin Towne.

1. We have a good and gen - tle Lord, Who gives us work to do;
2. Our hearts and hands be-long to him, He claims them as his own;
3. He keeps us here to bless the souls For whom his blood was shed,
4. And he has work in high - er spheres For lit - tle folks to do;

And   to the young-est comes the call, "The Lord hath need of you."
Our hands to do   his ho - ly will, Our hearts to   be his throne.
To scat-ter seeds of truth and love, And   in   his foot-steps tread.
And crowns of life and   joy di - vine, For   all   the good and true.

Chorus.

Then   let us love and serve him   well, And hon - or   his com-mands,

For   he is worth-y,   And he needs Both lit - tle hearts and hands.

No. 2. Little Pilgrims.

LEILA E. HODGSON.
With animation.

J. C. MACY.
Second Prize Piece.

1. We are hap-py lit-tle pil-grims, Go-ing on a journey home; There's a sweet voice
2. 'Tis the Lord who loves the chil-dren, Lit-tle ones like you and me; He has gone the
3. Tho' the way our Sav-ior leads us Will be of-ten dark and cold, We will fol-low

Chorus.

soft-ly call-ing, Ev-er call-ing us to come. We will fol-low, we will fol-low,
way be-fore us, Now he will our lead-er be. We will fol-low, etc.
in his foot-steps, Till we safe-ly reach the fold. We will fol-low, etc.

As we journey we will sing Songs of praises, songs of praises, To the Lord, our Savior King.

No. 3. Sabbath Day.

E. M. C.
Moderato.

E. MANFORD CLARK.

1. Let the chil-dren's voic-es blend, Sab-bath day, Sab-bath day, As thy
2. Type of fin-al rest a-bove, Sab-bath day, Sab-bath day, Welcome
3. Ho-ly and for-ev-er blest, Sab-bath day, Sab-bath day, How I

hymns of praise ascend, Sabbath day, Sabbath day; Day most ho-ly of the seven, Type of
all thy peace and love, Sabbath day, Sabbath day; Till our spir-it upward flies To its
love thy sacred rest, Sabbath day, Sabbath day; May these lit-tle feet of mine Ev-er

Sabbath Day—Concluded.

end - less rest in heaven, By the Lord di - vine - ly given, Sabbath day.
home be-yond the skies, May we all thy bless-ings prize, Sabbath day.
ev - er-more in - cline To the ho - ly and di - vine Sabbath day.

Chorus.

Sab-bath day, Sabbath day, Most ho - ly Sab-bath day.

Sabbath day, Sabbath day, Sabbath day, Most ho - ly Sabbath day.

No. 4. Jesus, I will Follow.

ADDIE TITUS.   C. P. HOFFMAN.

1. Je - sus, hold my lit - tle hand, Keep thou close by me,   Tho' I cannot
2. Je - sus, teach my lit - tle feet To walk the heavenly way,   May I love thee
3. Je - sus, watch my lit - tle tongue, May it nev - er say   An un-kind or
4. Je - sus, take me as I am, A sin - ful lit - tle one;   Thou wilt lead me

Chorus.

see thy face,   I will fol - low thee.   Je - sus, I will fol - low,
more and more, At night and ev - 'ry day.   Je - sus, I will, etc.
naught-y word, When I work or play.   Je - sus, I will, etc.
in - to heav'n, When my work is done.   Je - sus, I will, etc.

I will fol-low thee, Tho' I cannot see thy face, Thou wilt care for me.

No. 5. Home Above.

E. M. C.   E. Manford Clark.

1. There is a beau-ti-ful home Prepared for us   a-bove, Where none shall evermore
2.   I have a mansion up there, Which Je-sus keeps for me, And clean robes wait me up
3. They have no need of the sun   By day, or stars by night, For in   that beau-ti-ful

Chorus.

roam From God or from Je - sus' love.   Beautiful home   a - bove,   The
there When Jesus shall make me free.   Beautiful home   a - bove, etc.
home The Savior is all the light.   Beautiful home   a - bove, etc.

Beau-ti-ful, beau-ti-ful home up a-bove,

cit-y of mercy and love, There none shall evermore roam, Beautiful, beautiful home.

No. 6.   Guide Us, Loving Savior.

A. W. French   Minnie Minton.
                                                           Second Prize Piece.

1. Dear and lov-ing Sav - ior, Lis - ten to our prayer, Take us to   thy bo - som,
2. Kind and gen-tle Sav - ior, Guide us all the way, Keep thy lit - tle chil-dren
3. Hap - py, bless-ed Sav - ior, Thine we'll ev - er be,   As we on-ward jour-ney,

Keep us in   thy care;   We are lit - tle pil-grims, Wand'ring here be-low,
Near thee ev - 'ry day,   Lead us in   thy foot-steps, So we may not roam,
With sweet trust in thee,   For we know up yon - der, With thee, by and by,

Guide Us, Loving Savior—Concluded.

Chorus.

And we need thee, Je - sus,   Ev - 'ry-where we go.   Guide us, ev - er guide us,
Till we reach the man-sions   Of e - ter - nal home.   Guide us, etc.
We shall live for-ev - er,   In our home on high.   Guide us, etc.

Take us by the hand, Lead us, lov - ing Sav - ior, To the gold - en land.

No. 7.   Let Them Come to Me.

E. M. C.   E. MANFORD CLARK.

1. Children, hear the Sav - ior calling, "Let them come to me,   For of such is
2. Children, come then cheerfully To Je - sus' lov - ing arms,   He is call-ing
3. Children, Je - sus says to you, "Oh, come to me to - day,   Let the children

heav - en's kingdom, In its pu - ri - ty;"   Come and trust him and his grace Will
now for you, To shel - ter you from harm,   He will fold you in his arms, And
come to me, And keep them not a - way;"   Come to him then, while you may, (For

save you from all sin; Oh, children, seek the Savior's face, In ear - ly life be - gin.
draw you to his breast, He'll give to you a golden crown Of ev - er-last-ing rest.
time will soon be o'er), And you shall live in end-less day, With him for-ev-er-more.

No. 8. Say No!

O. D. Sherman.
C. E. Pollock.

1. If on some pleas-ant Sab-bath day, A play-mate un - to you should say, From
2. And if per-chance up - on the street, A wick-ed scorn-er you should meet, With
3. If Sa - tan ev - er pass-ing by, Should tempt to tell the smoothest lie, De-
4. And so of ev - 'ry path of sin, Your feet are prone to wan-der in, For

Chorus.

Sabbath-school let's stay a-way, And spend the hour in fun and play, Just say, No!) A
gracious words he would you greet, And wi-li - ly give you his seat; Just say, No! etc.
ceive your parents on the sly, Don't stop to ar-gue what or why; Just say, No! etc.
if the crown of life you'd win, An e - vil hab - it ne'er be - gin; Just say, No! etc.

good, round, hearty No! By this, true manliness you'll show, And honor God by say-ing No.

No. 9. Gifts for Jesus.

L. F. C.
Rev. L. F. Cole.

1. Dear Je - sus, we bring thee our off'rings to-day; We give thee our voic - es, ac-
2. Our eyes to be-hold thee in earth, sea, and sky, And see thee a-gain in the
3. Our minds too, to stud - y thy glo - ri - ous word, Our hear-ing to list to thy

cept them, we pray, Our hands for thy ser-vice, our feet for thy ways, Our
poor pass-er - by; Our hands to bring off'rings, and gifts for the poor, Our
voice, precious Lord; Our bod - ies thy tem - ple, our souls for thy throne, We

Gifts for Jesus—Concluded.

Chorus.

hearts for thy dwelling, our lips for thy praise. We bring gifts to Je-sus, We
hearts to swing o - pen to Je - sus the door, We bring gifts, etc.
bring thee ourselves, Lord, to be all thine own. We bring gifts, etc.

bring gifts to - day, Our all give thee, Je-sus, Ac - cept us, we pray.

No. 10.   How Jesus Feels.

Mrs. M. P. Smith.   C. E. Pollock.

1. When lit - tle chil-dren let sin - ful thoughts glow,   Let an-gry words from their
2. When they are fret - ful and cause oth - ers pain,   Self-ish and greed-y a-
3. When they tell falsehoods, are haugh-ty or vain,   When they his Sabbath both
4. All naughty thoughts I will put far a - way,   And I'll be gen-tle and

hearts ov-er-flow,   je-sus is sad;   When lit-tle children, no mat-ter how small,
gain and a-gain,   Je-sus is sad;   When they are kind to the weary and poor,
scorn and profane,   Je-sus is sad;   When they are try-ing his pre cepts to do,
kind ev-'ry day,   Lest he be sad; Yes, I will love him, my Sav-ior so kind,

Strive to be lov-ing and kind un-to all,   Je - sus is glad.
If they are pa-tient when pain they en-dure,   Je - sus is glad.
Lov-ing their par - ents, o - be - dient and true,   Je - sus is glad.
All his com-mand-ments en - deav - or to mind,   So he'll be glad.

No. 11. Jesus' Little Flock.

P. J. S.

P. J. SPRAGUE.

Sing with gentle voice.

1. Je - sus, we thy flock would be, Love, o - bey and fol-low thee, In the way which
2. Gentle Shepherd, hear our prayer, Grant us now thy ten - der care, Nev-er let us
3. Lead us gen-tly by the hand, To that bright and hap-py land Where the light of

Chorus.

thou hast trod, Leading upward to our God. Je - sus, we thy lit - tle flock,
go a - stray, Keep us in the King's highway. Je - sus, etc.
love u - lone, Shines from thy e - ter - nal throne. Je - sus, etc.

Would the path of du-ty walk, We, thy tender lambs, would be Nearer, Jesus, un-to thee.

No. 12. Praises.

L. F. C.

Rev. L. F. COLE.

Joyfully.

1. Birds are sing - ing, woods are ring - ing, With thy prais - es, bless - ed King;
2. Wa - ters danc-ing, sun-beams glanc-ing, Sing thy glo - ry cheer - i - ly;
3. An - gels o'er us join the cho - rus, Which on earth we sing to thee;

Lake and moun-tain, field and foun-tain, To thy throne their trib - utes bring.
Blos - soms break-ing, na - ture wak-ing, Chant thy prais - es mer - ri - ly.
Heaven is ring - ing, earth is sing - ing, Prais - es to thee joy - ful - ly.

Praises—Concluded.

Chorus.

We, thy chil-dren, join the cho-rus, Mer-ri-ly, cheer-i-ly, glad-ly

praise thee, Glad ho-san-nas, glad ho-san-nas, Joy-ful-ly we lift to thee.

No. 13. Little Christian Workers.

Mrs. A. H. Dixon.

E. A. Hoffman.

1. Who will come and take a stand, take a stand, take a stand, Join our lit-tle
2. Will you nev-er from him rove, from him rove, from him rove, Will you strive by
3. Come and join us, come and bring, come and bring, come and bring, Gifts be-fit-ting
4. Ev-'ry child some work can do, work can do, work can do, Be o-be-di-

hap-py band, hap-py band, hap-py band, Marching to the heavenly land,
works of love, works of love, works of love, Dear de-light in him to prove,
Christ our King, Christ our King, Christ our King, Youthful hearts that gladly sing,
ent and true, Be o-be-di-ent and true, Tell the sto-ry ev-er new,

Sing-ing softly, hand in hand, Singing songs, singing songs, Singing songs to Je-sus?
Who has gone to reign a-bove, reign a-bove, reign a-bove, Will you love this Je-sus?
Till the cho-ral arch-es ring, arch-es ring, arch-es ring, Ring with praise of Je-sus.
How he died for me and you, me and you, me and you, On the cross, dear Je-sus.

No. 14. Jesus Loves Us.

EBEN E. REXFORD.
Cheerfully.

W. IRVING HARTSHORN.
Second Prize Piece.

1. Je - sus loves us, Je - sus loves us, Lit - tle chil-dren long a - go,
2. Je - sus loves us, Je - sus loves us, We are pre-cious in his sight,
3. Je - sus loves us, Je - sus loves us, Let our hap - py hearts o'er - flow,
4. Je - sus loves us, Je - sus loves us, Oh, how glad we ought to be,

Came to him and found a bless - ing, We can come like them we know.
Let us prove our love to Je - sus, By our stead-fast-ness to right.
In a song of praise and glad - ness, That he car - eth for us so.
That he loves the lit - tle chil - dren, Lit - tle ones like you and me.

Chorus.

Je - sus loves us, Je - sus loves us, Sing with glad and grate - ful voice,

Je - sus loves the lit - tle chil - dren, Oh, be hap - py and re - joice!

No. 15. Hear Our Cry.

JNO. COLLINS.

W. H. H. SMITH.

1. Lov-ing Sav - ior! well we know, As we read the Bi - ble sto - ry,
2. Mighty Sav - ior! make us thine, Thine for time and thine for - ev - er,
3. Gen-tle Sav - ior! keep us pure, Kind and faith - ful to each oth - er,
4. Precious Sav - ior! may we know Thou hast all our sins for-giv - en,

Inst.

Hear Our Cry—Concluded.

Thou didst suf - fer long a - go, Lit - tle ones to come to thee,
Save us by thy power di - vine; Lest we wan - der from thy side,
Is not all thy prom-ise sure, Those who do thy will a - lone
Oh, that in this world be - low, We may all thy dear ones be,

And we would thy chil-dren be, That we may be-hold thy glo - ry.
Be our true and faith - ful guide, Thro' our life to death's cold riv - er.
Thou wilt ev - er call thine own, Moth - er, sis - ter, or thy broth-er?
Lov - ing and o - bey - ing thee, Till we sing thy praise in heav - en.

Chorus.

Je - sus, Sav - ior! hear our cry, Hear us from thy throne on high.

No. 16.   Our Father's Care.

HENRY M. DOUGLASS.   LEROY J. BOGGS.

1. God clothes the lil - ies of the field In rai - ment pure and white;
2. The ti - ny spar - row's lit - tle worth, He views with lov - ing eye;
3. He watch - eth o'er the chil - dren all, With ten - der - ness and skill,

He bids his peo - ple take the shield Of faith, and trust his might.
He guards the fee - ble ones of earth, And hears their faint - est cry.
And from their heads there may not fall One hair with-out his will.

No. 17. Praise the Lord.

C. E. P. *Spirited.*　　　　　　　　　　　　　　　　　　　　C. E. Pollock.

1. Lit - tle chil - dren, praise the Lord, Praise the Lord, praise the Lord,
2. Praise him for his bless - ed word, Bless - ed word, bless - ed word,
3. Praise him for the Sab - bath day, Sab - bath day, Sab - bath day,
4. Praise him for the Sun - day - school, Sun - day - school, Sun - day - school,
5. Praise him for your teach - ers dear, Teach - ers dear, teach - ers dear,

Lit - tle chil - dren praise the Lord, Praise ye the Lord.
Praise him for his bless - ed word, Praise ye the Lord.
Praise him for the Sab - bath day, Praise ye the Lord.
Praise him for the Sun - day-school, Praise ye the Lord.
Praise him for your teach - ers dear, Praise ye the Lord.

No. 18. Little Lambs.

M. M.　　　　　　　　　　　　　　　　　　　　　　　　Minnie Minton.

1. Lit-tle lambs of Christ are we, Safe-ly gathered in his fold, Where we dear-ly
2. Lit-tle lambs to him be-long, He will guard them day by day, He will help and
3. Lit-tle lambs need never fear, Je-sus loves them, this they know, There's for them a
4. Lit-tle lambs must ev-er sing, Of their Savior's precious love, As they to him

love to be, Sheltered from the storm and cold. Little lambs, little lambs,
make them strong, Seek them when they go a - stray. Little lambs, etc.
brighter sphere, Than this shad-ow - land be - low. Little lambs, etc.
fond - ly cling, Marching to the realm a - bove. Little lambs, etc.

Jesus keeps us in his care, Little lambs, little lambs, Near our Shepherd ev'rywhere.

E. M. C.   E. MANFORD CLARK.

1. Oh, how I love Je-sus, low-ly, meek and mild, He who gave his own life to
2. Oh, how I love Je-sus, love him all the day, Love the bless-ed Je-sus who
3. Oh, how I love Je-sus, love with all my soul, Love the bless-ed Je-sus and

save a lit-tle child; Oh, how I love Je-sus, God a-lone can tell.
takes my sins a-way, And takes this vile heart when black with sin-ful stain,
pray him make me whole; And pray that when I shall lay me down and die,

Chorus.

'Tis the name I love so well.   Oh, how I love to praise him, and
Makes it pure and white a-gain.   Oh, how I love, etc.
Je-sus take me up on high,   Oh, how I love, etc.

how I love to sing Of Je-sus, my Re-deem-er and King; Oh,

how I love Je-sus, u-ni-ver-sal King, Sav-ior of the world. A-men.

From "Primary Songs," by per.

No. 20. Let the Little Children Sing.

L. G. Wilson.   From "Primary S. S. Teacher," by per.   Mary C. Wilson.

1. Je-sus died on Cal-va-ry, All our debt to pay, May we all some tribute bring,
2. Children never should forget They have work to do; In the Master's vineyard yet,
3. Children, you have souls to save, For the home above; Lives to live beyond the grave,
4. Je-sus, while on earth, you know, Was the children's friend, And if you to heaven would go,

On this Sabbath day; Lit-tle children, too, may come, You may sing and pray;
There is room for you; You can teach the golden rule, When about your play;
With the friends you ove; Do not fail that home to gain, Where we all may rest,
Must not him of-fend; You must all his will o-bey, Humbly ask him how;

Chorus.

You may each and ev-'ry one, Bless this ho-ly day. Let the lit-tle children sing,
Bring new scholars to our school, On each Sabbath day. Let the lit-tle, etc.
Free from sorrow, free from pain, Ev-er with the blest. Let the lit-tle, etc.
He will guide you day by day, He will help you now. Let the lit-tle, etc.

Let the lit-tle children pray; Praising thus our heavenly King, On this sa-cred day.

No. 21. I am Little.

J. E. H.   From "Primary S. S. Teacher," by per.   J. E. Hall.   *Prize Piece.*

1. I am lit-tle, but I love, I love Je-sus, he loves me; I am lit-tle, but I
2. I am lit-tle, but I sing, Sing of him who came to save; I am lit-tle, but I
3. I am lit-tle, but I pray, Je-sus lis-tens, he is nigh; I am lit-tle, but I
4. I am lit-tle, but I hope Up in heaven at last to dwell; I am lit-tle, but I

I am ⸱Little—Concluded.

Chorus.

love Near his precious side to be.
sing, Now his par-don I may have.
pray, And he hears my humble cry.
hope, There for aye his praise to tell.

I am lit-tle, Je-sus knows, For he
I am lit-tle, etc.
I am lit-tle, etc.
I am lit-tle, etc.

sees me ev-'ry day; I am lit-tle Je-sus knows, So he leads me all the way.

No. 22. Little Words of Kindness.

Lively.

From " Primary S. S. Teacher," by per.

G. E POLLOCK.
Prize Piece.

1. Lit-tle words of kind-ness, Whispered soft and low, With a thrill of
2. Lit-tle words of kind-ness, Lo, a work of love, God's own hand re-
3. Lit-tle deeds of kind-ness, Heart-i-ly be-stowed, Help a faint-ing
4. Lit-tle words of kind-ness Seem of lit-tle worth, Yet we can-not

glad-ness, To the heart they go, Light-ing up its dark-ness,
cords them In the world a-bove; They whose words of pit-y
broth-er On life's wea-ry road; Lit-tle deeds of kind-ness
buy them With the gold of earth; Scat-ter, then, like sun-beams,

With a cheer-ing ray, Changing heav-y sad-ness To the light of day.
Dry the mourner's tears, Have the Sav-ior's bless-ing Thro' their earth-ly years.
To a wand'ring soul, Blessed by God, may lead him Back to Je-sus' fold.
Many a word of love, And the Lord of heav-en, Bless you from a-bove.

No. 23. A Little Child.

P. J. S.

From "Primary S. S. Teacher," by per.

P. J. SPRAGUE.
Prize Piece.

1. A lit-tle child I know I am, But still I love to sing The prais-es of the
2. I love the song that tells me how The Savior died for me, How on the cru-el
3. I hope to join that cho-ral song, With angels in the sky, And to the heavenly

Chorus.

Son of Man, My Sav-ior and my King. Lit-tle child, little child I am, I am the
cross he paid The debt that sets me free. Lit-tle child, etc.
host be-long, With Je-sus up on high. Lit-tle child, etc.

Savior's lit-tle lamb; Little child, little child I am, I am the Savior's lit-tle lamb.

No. 24. I'm a Little Pilgrim.

J. C. M

From "Primary S. S. Teacher," by per.

J. C. MACY.
Prize Piece.

1. I'm a lit-tle pilgrim, And I'll march along, Doing what I can for Je-sus;
2. I'm a lit-tle pilgrim, Working for the right, Do-ing lit-tle deeds for Je-sus;
3. I'm a lit-tle pilgrim, Telling ev-'ry one All about the love of Je-sus;

For he loves me dear-ly, And he'll make me strong, If I put my trust in him.
Won't you come and help me, Walking in the light? Come, and put your trust in him.
When my journey's end-ed, And my work is done, Christ will take me home to him.

I'm a Little Pilgrim—Concluded.

Chorus.

I'm a lit - tle pil - grim, yes, yes, yes! Come and see, come and see

How the heavenly Fa - ther loves to bless Lit - tle chil-dren just like me!

No. 25. Little Light.

From "Primary S. S. Teacher," by per.

C. E. Pollock.

Prize Piece.

1. God make my life a lit - tle light, With-in this world to glow; A lit - tle flame that
2. God make my life a sin-gle flower, That giv- eth joy to all, Con-tent to bloom in
3. God make my life a lit - tle song, That com fort - eth the sad, That help eth oth - ers
4. God make my life a lit - tle hymn Of ten - der-ness and praise; Of faith that nev - er

burn-eth bright Wher-ev - er I may go. Little light, little light, Wher-
na-tive bower, Although its place be small. Little light, etc.
to be strong, And makes the singer glad. Little light, etc.
wax-eth dim, In all his wondrous ways. Little light, etc.

Little light, little light,

Chorus.

ev - er I may go; Lit-tle light, lit-tle light, Wher-ev - er I may go.

Lit-tle light, lit-tle light,

No. 26. We'll Not Give Up the Bible.

From "Primary S. S. Teacher," by per.

C. E. Pollock.

1. We'll not give up the Bi - ble, God's ho - ly book of truth, The bless-ed staff of
2. We'll not give up the Bi - ble, For pleas-ure or for pain, We'll buy the truth and
3. We'll not give up the Bi - ble, But spread it far and wide, Un - til its sav - ing

hoar - y age, The guide of ear - ly youth; The sun that sheds a glorious light O'er
sell it not For all that we might gain ; Tho' man should try to take our prize, By
voice be heard Be-yond the roll-ing tide; Till all shall know its graciouspower, And

ev - 'ry drear - y road, The voice which speaks a Sav-ior's love, And
guile or cru - el might, We'll suf - fer all that men can do, And
with one voice and heart Re - solve that from God's sa - cred word, We

Chorus.

brings us home to God. We'll not give up the Bi - ble, God's ho - ly book of
God defend the right. We'll not give up the Bi - ble, etc.
nev - er, nev - er, part. We'll not give up the Bi - ble, etc.

truth, The bless - ed staff of hoar - y age, The guide of ear - ly youth.

No. 27. Something to Do.

From "Primary S.S. Teacher," by per.

ADDIE TITUS.
Prize Piece.

1. There is something on earth for the children to do, Ere they go to the beau-ti-ful land; There's a path-way of love where the young-est may go, And em-ploy-ment for each lit-tle hand.

2. Tho' it may be but lit-tle, our Sav-ior once said, If the lit-tle be giv-en in love, To the thirst-y a drink, to the hun-gry some bread, 'Twill be sure-ly re-ward-ed a-bove.

3. And the children can tell the sweet sto-ry of old, Tell of Him by whom sin is for-giv'n; And the an-gels of God will re-joice if one soul Should be led by the chil-dren to heaven.

Chorus.

There is something to do, there is something to do, There is something for chil-dren to do; To lead oth-ers to love the dear Sav-ior a-bove, There is something for children to do.

There is something, etc.
There is something, etc.

No. 28. Little Ones.

From " Primary S. S. Teacher," by per.

T. Martin Towne.
Prize Piece.

1. Je - sus loves the lit - tle ones, Loves to have us near; Close be-side him
2. We are like the lit - tle lambs, Sheltered in the fold, Je - sus is the
3. Lambs should never seek to stray From the Shepherd's side, If they wan-der
4. If the way is wea - ri - some, And we long for rest, Then he bears us

Chorus.

we will keep, Walk-ing with-out fear, Je - sus loves the lit - tle ones,
Shepherd kind, Keep-ing us from cold. Je - sus loves, etc.
far from him, E - vil will be-tide. Je - sus loves, etc.
in his arms, Next his lov-ing breast. Je - sus loves, etc.

O may we love him; May we ev - er heed his voice When we're led to sin.

No. 29. Jesus is the Friend of Children.

Rev. D. P. Gurley.

From " Primary S. S. Teacher," by per.

C. E. Pollock.

1. Je - sus is the friend of chil - dren, Je - sus is the friend of chil - dren,
2. Je - sus is our faith-ful teach - er, Je - sus is our faith-ful teach - er,
3. Je - sus suffered to re-deem us, Je - sus suffered to re-deem us,
4. Je - sus pleads for us in heav - en, Je - sus pleads for us in heav - en,
5. None but Je-sus, none but Je - sus, None but Je-sus, none but Je - sus,

Je - sus is the friend of chil - dren, We praise him for his love;
Je - sus is our faith-ful teach - er, We praise him for his word;
Je - sus suffered to re-deem us, We praise him for his cross;
Je - sus pleads for us in heav - en, We praise him for his plea;
None but Je - sus, none but Je - sus, Shall have our hearts' best love;

Jesus is the Friend of Children—Concluded.

He will lead us home to glo - ry,   He will lead us home to glo - ry,
We will heed his lov-ing coun - sel, We will heed his lov-ing coun - sel,
All the charms that sin can of - fer, All the charms that sin can of - fer,
Faith - ful ad - vo-cate, we'll praise him, Faith - ful ad-vo-cate, we'll praise him,
He will lead us home to glo - ry,   He will lead us home to glo - ry.

He will lead us home to glo - ry,   His own bright home a - bove.
We will heed his lov-ing coun - sel, The coun - sel of the Lord.
All the charms that sin can of - fer, For him we count but loss.
Faith - ful ad - vo-cate, we'll praise him Thro' all e - ter - ni - ty.
He will lead us home to glo - ry,   His own bright home a - bove.

No. 30. Gentle Savior.

From Primary S. S. Teacher, by per.

C. E. POLLOCK.
Prize Piece.

1. Je - sus, gen-tle Sav - ior,   Ev - er meek and mild,   In thy ten - der
2. Like a gen-tle Shep-herd   Lead me all the day,   Sav-ior, do not
3. With the birds that praise thee, Sing - ing in the shade, And the streams re -

mer - cy,   Hear a   lit - tle child;   Teach me how to love thee,
leave me, Let me   nev - er stray;   When my steps are wea - ry,
joic - ing, With all thou hast made, Je - sus, I would praise thee.

Teach me how to pray, Whis-per to my spir - it, Tell me what to say.
Lay me on thy breast, Sweet will be my slum - ber, Peace-ful there my rest.
In my joy - ful song, Of thy lov-ing kind - ness, Sing-ing all day long.

No. 31. Savior, Lead Us All the Way.

E. R. Latta.

A. B. Condo.

1. Lit - tle hearts from thee may wan - der, Lit - tle feet may go a - stray;
2. Lit - tle hands may yield to e - vil, Lit - tle lips wrong words may say;
3. Lit - tle chil - dren, like the flow-'rets, Oh, how oft in death de - cay!
4. To the ev - er - last - ing man-sions, Where the an - gel chil-dren stay,

That we in thy steps may fol - low, Sav - ior, lead us all the way.
Blest Re - deem-er, save the chil - dren, Sav - ior, lead us all the way.
Lord, pro - tect them while they lin - ger, Sav - ior, lead us all the way.
Let us all at last be gath-ered, Sav - ior, lead us all the way.

Chorus.

Day by day; yes, day by day, Sav - ior, lead us all the way.

Day by day; yes, day by day, Sav - ior, lead us all the way.

No. 32. Happy Child.

P. J. S.

From "Primary S. S. Teacher," by per

P. J. Sprague.

1. Je-sus, make me low - ly, Gen-tle, meek and mild; Lov-ing, trust-ing,
2. Je-sus, let thy Spir - it, In a gen - tle voice, Speak so I can
3. Je-sus, may I nev - er Lose my zeal and love; Let me live for-

Happy Child—Concluded.

Chorus.

ho - ly, Hap - py, lit - tle child. Hap-py child, rec - on - ciled
hear it Say to me re - joice. Hap-py child, etc.
ev - er In thy home a - bove. Hap-py child, etc.

To the God of love; Now I know I may go To his home a - bove.

No. 33.   Jesus, Blessed Jesus.

J. E. H.   From "Primary S. S. Teacher," by per.   J. E. HALL.

1. Now to thee our voic - es raise, Je - sus, bless-ed Je - sus; Thou art worth-y
2. Glad we sing our lit - tle songs, Je - sus, lov - ing Je - sus; Un - to thee their
3. Tune our voic-es sweet and clear, Je - sus, precious Je - sus; May their mu-sic
4. May we hear thy lov - ing "Come," Je - sus, pleading Je - sus; And at last, be

Chorus.

of all praise, Je - sus, bless-ed Je - sus. We would praise thee and a - dore,
praise be-longs, Je - sus, lov - ing Je - sus. We would praise, etc.
reach thine ear, Je - sus, pre-cious Je - sus. We would praise, etc.
gath-ered home, Je - sus, pleading Je - sus. We would praise, etc.

We would praise thee evermore, Hear us now we do implore, Je-sus, blessed Je - sus.

No. 34. I Rather Would Tell Them to Jesus.

Ellen Oliver.

M. A. Rubles.
Third Prize Piece.

1. I rather would tell them to Je - sus, To Je - sus so gen-tle and mild,
2. The Sav-ior a-way up in heav - en, Looks down on the children at play,
3. I think that he always re - mem-bers His childhood, so long, long a - go,
4. He pit - ies our lit-tle temp - ta - tions, And mourns for the wrongs that we do;

The sins I'm so of - ten com-mit - ting, For Je - sus was tru-ly a child.
And ev - er is ten-der - ly watch - ing, To guard us from go-ing a - stray.
And thinks of his wayward companions, When naughty and fretful we grow.
He'll curb all our childish im-pa-tience, If we pray to him humble and true.

Chorus.

I know I've a Sav-ior in heav - en, Whose blessings for-ev-er de - scend;

My sins I would car-ry to Je - sus, To Je-sus, the children's dear Friend.

No. 35. Two Little Hands.

W. A. O.

W. A. Ogden.
First Prize Piece.

1. I've two lit-tle hands to work for Je - sus, One lit-tle tongue his praise to tell,
2. I've two lit-tle feet to tread the path-way Up to the heavenly courts a - bove;
3. I've one lit-tle heart to give to Je - sus, One lit-tle soul for him to save,

Two Little Hands—Concluded.

Two lit-tle ears to hear his coun-sel, One lit-tle voice a song to swell.
Two lit-tle eyes to read the Bi - ble, Tell - ing of Je - sus' wondrous love.
One lit-tle life for his dear ser-vice, One lit tle self that he must have.

Chorus.

1ST TIME.   2D TIME.

Lord, we come, Lord, we come, In our childhood's early morning, Come to learn of thee.

No. 36. Little Feet.

ARTHUR J. HODGES.   From "Primary S.S. Teacher," by per.   LEROY J. BOGGS.

Not too fast.

1. Lit-tle feet are wea - ry, Wea-ry and so sore; But the Lord can give them
2. Lit-tle feet have wandered, Wandered far a - way; But the Lord can bring them
3. Lit - tle feet have trod - den, Trodden ways of sin; But the Lord can cleanse them
4. Lit - tle feet in troub - le, Je - sus is a friend; Sin shall nev - er van-quish,

Chorus.

Rest for - ev - er - more.   Bless - ed Sav-ior, bless - ed Lord! Bless - ed Bi - ble,
To a bright-er day.   Bless - ed Sav-ior, etc.
That they en - ter in.   Bless - ed Sav-ior, etc.
For he will de - fend.   Bless - ed Sav-ior, etc.

ho - ly word; Bless-ed hope to mor-tals given—Hope of rest, sweet rest in heaven.

No. 37. Jesus, Bless Us.

Miss R. HUBER.　　　　　　　　　　　　　　　　PHIL A. HUBER.

With animation.

1. Je - sus, gen - tle Shep-herd,　Bless thy lambs to - day,　Keep them in thy
2. Help us sing thy prais - es,　Help us do thy will,　And to o - ver-

foot - steps,　Nev - er let them stray;　Bless the lit - tle chil - dren,
flow - ing,　Ev - 'ry heart now fill;　Make us lit - tle sol - diers,

Teach them how to pray,　Keep their feet from stray-ing From the nar-row way.
Fight - ing for the right,　And with prayer and praising, Keep our ar-mor bright.

No. 38. Christmas Carol.

E. B. S.　　　　　　　　　　　　　　　　　　　E. B. SMITH.

1. A star shone in the heav - ens　On Christ-mas morn,　Above the place where
2. The wise men saw its bright - ness, And came from far,　They found the way to
3. Oh, may this star of beau - ty　Still point the way　To lead us all to

Chorus.

Je - sus,　The Lord, was born.　O ho - ly, ho - ly Christ-mas,　O
Je - sus,　Led by the star.　O ho - ly, etc.
Je - sus,　This Christ-mas day.　O ho - ly, etc.

Christmas Carol—Concluded.

bless-ed, blessed Christ-mas, O joy-ful, joy-ful Christmas, When Christ was born.

No. 39. Something for You.

MARGARETTE SNODGRASS.

C. E. POLLOCK.

1. Lit-tle ones, lit-tle ones, Stop and think, What have you done for Je - sus?
2. Ev-er wide o-pen, then, Keep your eyes, Watch-ing some work for Je - sus;
3. Lit-tle ones, fresh with the morn-ing dew, Joy - ful - ly work for Je - sus,
4. Glad lit-tle hearts, if you on - ly knew What you could do for Je - sus,

Al-ways you see, For you and me, There's something to do for Je - sus.
Always you know, Where e'er you go, There's much to be done for Je - sus;
Heav - y or light, All will come right, If done for the love of Je - sus.
With a glad voice Heaven would rejoice, So much would be done for Je - sus.

Chorus.

Brave lit-tle hearts, you must not de-lay, There is so much to do to - day;

E - ven a word, It may be heard Up at the throne of Je - sus.

No. 40. The Care of Jesus.

Cheerfully.

C. A. FYKE.

Third Prize Piece.

1. Lov-ing-ly the bless-ed Sav-ior Draws us near-er to his breast,
2. Ten-der-ly the bless-ed Sav-ior Watch-es o'er us day by day,
3. Will-ing-ly, oh, bless-ed Sav-ior, We will trust in thee a-lone,

Hap-py now are all the chil-dren, Shel-tered in his arms to rest.
Lest our ev-er err-ing foot-steps Wan-der from the heavenly way.
To be guid-ed in the jour-ney To our ev-er-last-ing home.

Chorus.

Ten-der-ly and lov-ing-ly Lead us in the bet-ter way;

Will-ing-ly and cheer-ful-ly We'll be guid-ed day by day.

No. 41. Blessing the Little Ones.

EBEN E. REXFORD.

D. B. WAT.

1. I love to think of Je-sus, With the chil-dren at his knee,
2. And when I read the sto-ry, He seems be-side me here,
3. In paths that lead to heav-en Our youth-ful feet are set,

Blessing the Little Ones—Concluded.

And oft, in thought-ful mo-ments, His outstretched arms I see;
I feel his eyes up-on me With-out a thought of fear,
But we are prone to wan-der, To prom-ise and for-get;

I hear his words of bless-ing A-bove each lit-tle head,
Be-cause I know he loves me, And on my head he lays
But if this sweet, sweet sto-ry May lin-ger in my heart,

And I am filled with glad-ness Re-mem-bering what he said:
His ho-ly hands in bless-ing, As in the old-en days.
From him who loved the chil-dren My feet will ne'er de-part.

Chorus.

"O! suf-fer lit-tle chil-dren," Je-sus said, "to come to Me,

For of such shall heav-en's king-dom, Heaven's hap-py king-dom be."

No. 42. Gentle Jesus.

ANNIE R. JOHNSON.

C. P. HOFFMANN.

First Prize Piece.

1. Gen - tle Je - sus, gen - tle Je - sus, Bless thy lit - tle ones to-day;
2. Should the wolves of sin howl round us, Still we know we need not fear,
3. Gen - tle Je - sus, ten - der Shep-herd, Thou wilt keep us safe from harm,
4. Oh! it is not strange we love him, For he shed his sin - less blood,

Shel - ter us from harm, dear Shepherd, Watch us, keep us in the way.
While our might - y Shepherd guards us, Bid - ding us to flock more near.
Should a lit - tle lamb grow wea - ry, Thou wilt bear it on thine arm.
Just to give us peace and par - don, Pre - cious, pre - cious Lamb of God.

Chorus.

To thee we be-long, We cannot go wrong While Jesus, our Shepherd, thus leads us along,

To thee we belong, We cannot go wrong While Jesus, our Shepherd, thus leads us along.

No. 43. Jesus Watches O'er Me.

Rev. J. B. ATCHINSON.

W. IRVING HARTSHORN.

First Prize Piece.

1. Je - sus sees me ev-'ry day, When I work and when I play, When I laugh and
2. When I'm naughty, when I'm good, When I'm pleasant, when I'm rude, Everywhere I
3. When he is so kind to me, What a good child I should be; Make me bet - ter

Jesus Watches O'er Me—Concluded.

Chorus.

when I weep, When I wake and when I sleep. Je - sus watches o'er me,
stay or go, 'Tis be-cause he loves me so. Je - sus watches, etc.
Lord, I pray, And re-mem-ber day by day, Je - sus watches, etc.

Je - sus watches o'er me; O how glad I am to know Je - sus watches o-ver me.

No. 44. The Morning Star.

Rev. Rob't Kerr.
Happily.

W. Irving Hartshorn.

1. How sweetly Christ, the morning star Shines on our pilgrim way, To guide us thro' the
2. When tossed on life's wide heaving sea, Where tempests wildly rave, His beams bring cheer and
3. The beauteous star that shines on us Foretells the dawn of day, Be - fore whose face all

Chorus.

night of time To heaven's unclouded day. To him we raise our grateful song, Whose
ban-ish fear, And gild the troubled wave. To him we raise, etc.
e - vil things Shall swiftly flee a - way. To him we raise, etc.

glo - ry from a - far Makes glad our hearts and lights our path, The bright and Morning Star.

No. 45. Savior, Bless Me.

EBEN E. REXFORD.　　　　　　　　　　　　　　　J. H. TENNEY.

1. Sav - ior, bless me, let me be Ev - er - more a child of thine;
2. Draw me clos - er ev - 'ry day, To the heart that lov - eth me;
3. Give me strength to do for thee Some - thing that shall part re - pay
4. Grant me, Sav - ior, at the last, When the crowns of life are given,

Drawn by love and trust to thee, Lead me in the way di - vine.
I am sure to go a - stray If I can - not cling to thee.
All the love thou giv - est me In life's jour - ney day by day.
And the work of earth is past, Home and rest with thee in heaven.

Refrain.

Je - sus, take me by the hand, Lead me to the Bet - ter Land;

Je - sus, take me by the hand, Lead me to the Bet - ter Land.

No. 46. Jesus, Gentle Savior.

O. W. B.　　　　　　　　　　　　　　　　　　　　O. W. BONNEY.
Second Prize Words.

1. Je - sus, gen - tle Sav - ior, Hear me as I pray; Take my sin and
2. I am weak and sin - ful, Fail - ing ev - 'ry day; Oh, how much I

Jesus, Gentle Savior—Concluded.

sor - row, Take my guilt a - way. Make me pure and ho - ly,
need thee, Teach me how to pray. Teach me in my weak - ness

More and more like thee; In the hour of tri - al, Be thou near to me.
How I may be strong; Keep me, O my Sav - ior, Ev - er from the wrong.

No. 47. Pilgrim Band.

D. A. B.   DELLA A. BROWN.

1. We're a lit - tle pil - grim band, March-ing on, march-ing on;
2. Je - sus loves the lit - tle ones, This we know, this we know;
3. E'en the least can some-thing do, Tho' 'tis small, tho' 'tis small;

Chorus.

Marching to the bet-ter land, Glo-ry is our song. Come, then, join this happy band,
For 'tis Je-sus tells us so In his ho - ly word. Come, then, etc.
All who fol-low at his call, Safe with him shall dwell. Come, then, etc.

Je-sus takes you by the hand; When around his throne we stand, We'll praise him evermore.

No. 48. This is the Sweetest Story.

MARGARETTE SNODGRASS.

C. E. POLLOCK.

Third Prize Piece.

1. This is the sweet-est sto - ry, Won-der - ful, strange and true,
2. Think you not, "He's for - got - ten, It was so long a - go."
3. Know-ing a child's temp-ta - tions, Show-ing you what to do,

Je - sus, the King of glo - ry, Once was a child like you.
No, the dear Lord re - mem - bers, Oh! and he loves you so;
Je - sus will stand be - side you, Mak-ing you brave and true;

Think of him in your glad-ness, Praising him all the day, Ev-er in words and
Loves you for aye and ev - er, It was to you he came; Deep in his heart is
Ev - er keep closely to him, If you would like him grow, Out of your heart's deep

Chorus.

ac - tions, Think what the Lord would say. Always be bright and joy - ous,
grav - en Ev - er - y child-ish name. Always be bright, etc.
glad - ness Sweetness of life will flow. Always be bright, etc.

Jesus would have you so; He is the source of gladness, He is the light, you know.

No. 49. Little Children.

Mrs. F. A. Blaisdell.   Frank M. Davis.

1st voice or duet.

1. Je - sus loves the lit - tle chil - dren With a ver - y ten - der love,
2. The good Bi - ble tells us plain - ly, He who reads may clear - ly see;
3. He that gives a cup of wa - ter To a lit - tle one in love,
4. "Feed my lambs," he said to Pe - ter, "If you love me as you say,
5. And he said to his dis - ci - ples, Warn - ing them of pride and sin,
All. 6. Help us, then, O bless - ed Sav - ior, As we old - er grow each day,

And our lips should chant his prais - es, Ev - 'ry oth - er name a - bove.
He said, "Suf - fer lit - tle chil - dren, Let them come right un - to me."
He shall sure - ly be re - ward - ed, By my Fa - ther from a - bove.
Feed my lambs." He knew they'd hun - ger, Climb - ing up the heavenly way.
"Ye must be like lit - tle chil - dren, If my home you'd en - ter in."
Still to be thy lit - tle chil - dren, Walking where thou lead'st the way.

Chorus.

Hal - le - lu - jah, Hal - le - lu - jah, High our prais - es shall as -
cend; Hal - le - lu - jah, hal - le - lu - jah, To the lit - tle chil - dren's

2d voice.

Friend. How do you know he loves us so? Who told you, say?
Ah, that is sweet, yet more re - peat Of his kind words.
And is that all you can re - call? Oh, tell us more.
O, dear Je - sus, bless - ed Je - sus! Oh, tell us more.

No. 50. The Children's Friend.

E. E. Starkey.

Dr. J. B. Herbert.

1. How blest and hap - py must have been The chil - dren long a - go,
2. How gra - cious must his smile have seemed, How gen - tle all his ways;
3. We may not hear on earth his voice, His face we may not see,
4. And if we live as he has taught, His arms will bear us home;

Their Sav - ior's lov - ing arms with - in, Their Sav - ior's voice to know.
How heav - en - ly the light that beamed On them from his dear eyes.
But we may in his love re - joice, And in his pres - ence be.
For Je - sus said, "For - bid them not, But suf - fer them to come."

Chorus.

The Sav - ior is the children's friend, He will for - sake us nev - er,

Then let us sing our Sav - ior, King, And love and serve him ev - er.

No. 51. Christ at Bethlehem.

W. S. B. M.

(Christmas Carol.)

W. S. B. Mathews, by per.

Solo.

1. Long a - go on Christmas night, Shepherds saw the heav'nly light, Heard the song of
2. Quick to Bethlehem, they, to see What the an - gels' joy could be; Lo! for love of
3. Come with them to sacred stall, On our knees with wise men fall; Sav - ior, King, and

Christ at Bethlehem—Concluded.

Chorus.

an-gels bright, Christ was born at Bethlehem. Christ, our King, Christ, our King,
you and me, Christ was born at Bethlehem. Christ, our King, etc.
Lord of all, Christ was born at Bethlehem. Christ, our King, etc.

Ev'ry voice his praise shall sing, Jesus Christ our Lord and King, Came that day to Bethlehem.

No. 52. Tell Me All About Jesus.

Rev. Elisha A. Hoffman. Joseph Garrison.

1. Tell me all a-bout Je - sus, Who came from heav'n above; Tell me more of his
2. Tell me all a-bout Je - sus, The Lamb of Cal - va - ry; Tell me more of his
3. Tell me all a-bout Je - sus, Who dai - ly cares for me; Tell me why he should
4. Tell me all a-bout Je - sus, Re - peat the sto - ry o'er, Nev - er shall I grow

Chorus.

good - ness, More of his pre-cious love. Tell me all a-bout Je - sus, Tell
mer - cy, More of his grace to me. Tell me, etc.
love me, Why he should die for me. Tell me, etc.
wea - ry, Hear-ing it more and more. Tell me, etc.

me that I may know, The sto - ry of the Sav - ior, Who loves, who loves me so.

No. 53. Suffer the Children to Come to Me.

MARGARETTE SNODGRASS.   From "Primary S. S. Teacher," by per.   J. M. S., by per.

1. The sweetest words I have ev-er read Are the loving words that the Savior said:
2. Oh, how he parted the throng that pressed, And so tenderly ev-'ry child caressed!
3. I wonder what I should ev-er do, If the Sav-ior had on-ly called a few;
4. I grieve to think I should ev-er go Far away from Him who has loved me so;

"Suf - fer the chil-dren to come to me." Who would ever thought of this but He?
This is the glad-ness of all my song, That to this dear Sav - ior I be-long
Tak - ing the old, and the wise and great, Oh, I am so glad I need not wait.
All thro' my life this my song shall be, What the blessed Sav-ior's done for me.

Chorus.

"Suf - fer the children to come to me," "Suf-fer the children to come to me;"

I am as glad as glad can be, Those ver-y words were meant for me.

No. 54. Sing to the King.

MARGARETTE SNODGRASS.   From "Good Will," by per.   T. MARTIN TOWNE.

1. Sing, oh, sing, Lit-tle ones sing; Prais-es bring Un-to the King, Prais-es bring
2. Glad-ly beat, Little hearts, beat; Love so sweet Lay at his feet, Love so sweet
3. Up and do, Little hearts, true; Days are few, Even for you, Days are few,

Sing to the King—Concluded.

Chorus.

Un-to the King, Un-to the King of Glo - ry!   Un-to the King of Glo - ry,
Lay at his feet, Happy hearts full of treas - ure.   Un - to the King, etc.
Even for you; Up and be ev - er do - ing.   Un - to the King, etc.

Loud let the glad notes ring, let them ring ; Unto the King of Glory Loud let the glad notes ring.

No. 55. Love Each Other.

ELISHA A. HOFFMAN.   From "Happy Songs," by per.   R. B. MAHAFFEY.

1. Lit-tle chil-dren, love each other, With af-fec-tion warm and true, Always try to
2. Lit-tle chil-dren, love each other, Nev - er cause a heart to pain; Tho' you meet with
3. Lit-tle chil-dren, love each other, You will always find it best, For in being

Chorus.

do to oth - ers, As you'd have them do to you.   Try to do, try to do,
great un-kind-ness, Do not be un-kind a - gain.   Try to do, etc.
kind to oth - ers, You will be su-preme-ly blest.   Try to do, etc.

Un - to oth-ers try to do,   As you would, as you would They should do to you

No. 56. Let the Children Sing.

BLUE BELL.   F. H. H. THOMSON.

1. I know the bless-ed Sav - ior Who dwells in heaven a - bove, Doth
2. And when he came from heav - en To live with men be - low, He
3. And if we love the Sav - ior, And serve him ev - 'ry day, If

lis - ten when the chil - dren Sing of his dy - ing love. He loves to hear their
loved the lit - tle chil - dren, And of - ten told them so. And once, with - in the
from the path of du - ty We nev - er go a - stray, When life for us is

voic - es, So hap - py, mer - ry, clear, Attuned to sing his prais - es With
tem - ple, When they be - gan to sing, He said their praise was per - fect, "Ho-
o - ver, And we are called a - way, We'll sing his praise in heav - en, Where

Chorus.

those who serve him here. Then let our voic-es min-gle With songs the an-gels
san - na to the King." Then let our voic-es, etc.
bless-ed an - gels stay. Then let our voic-es, etc.

sing, "Ho - san - na in the high - est, Ho - san - na to the King."

No. 57. We are Little Gleaners.

CHAS. H. GABRIEL

1. We are lit-tle gleaners brave, Toil-ing all the day, In the vineyard
2. We are lit-tle gleaners brave, In the vineyard wide, There is work for
3. We are lit-tle gleaners brave, Harvest-time goes by, Come and help there's

of the Lord, Bear-ing sheaves a-way; Faith-ful gleaners will we prove,
all to do, There will we a-bide; Tares are scattered ev-ry-where,
room for all, Stand not i-dly by; All the faith-ful, val-iant band,

Trust-ing in our Sav-ior's love; We are lit-tle glean-ers brave,
We must search them out with care; We are lit-tle glean-ers brave,
Christ will crown in glo-ry-land; We are lit-tle glean-ers brave,

Chorus.

Glean-ing for the Lord. Lit-tle gleaners for the Lord, Hap-py we,
Glean-ing for the Lord. Lit-tle gleaners, etc.
Glean-ing for the Lord. Lit-tle gleaners, etc.

hap-py we, Gleaning in the field so broad, Gleaning for the Lord.

No. 58. Happy Hearts.

MATA WILSON.
Cheerfully.

C. A. FYKE.

1. I'm glad the gold-en sun-light Is shining o'er our way, And na-ture seems so
2. The perfume of the flow-ers Floats upward to the sky; The birds are sing-ing
3. And if the birds and flow-ers All praise the Lord our King, I'm sure the lit-tle

Chorus.

hap-py, This ho-ly Sab-bath day. Dear Fa-ther, we will praise thee, This
prais-es To God who dwells on high. Dear Fa-ther, etc.
chil-dren A song of praise may bring. Dear Fa-ther, etc.

hap-py, hap-py day, For 'tis thy lov-ing-kind-ness That brightens all our way.

No. 59. He Loves Me, Too.

MARIA STRAUB.
From "Crown of Glory," by per.
S. W. STRAUB.

1. God sees the lit-tle spar-row fall, It meets his ten-der view;
2. He paints the lil-y of the field, Per-fumes each lil-y bell;
3. God made the lit-tle birds and flow'rs, And all things large and small;

If God so loves the lit-tle birds, I know he loves me, too.
If he so loves the lit-tle flow'rs, I know he loves me well.
He'll not for-get his lit-tle ones, I know he loves them all.

He Loves Me, Too—Concluded.

Chorus.

He loves me, too, He loves me, too, I know he loves me, too;

Be - cause he loves the lit - tle things, I know he loves me, too.

No. 60. What a Friend the Children Have.

Rev. Jno. Parker.   Karl Reden.

Moderato.

1. What a friend the chil-dren have, children have, chil-dren have, What a friend the
2. What a friend the chil-dren have, children have, chil-dren have, What a friend the
3. What a friend the chil-dren have, children have, chil-dren have, What a friend the
4. Should not all the chil-dren sing, children sing, chil-dren sing, Should not all the

chil-dren have   In the Sav-ior's love;   Walks be-side them, Gen - tly chides them
chil-dren have   In the Sav-ior's power;   He de-fends them And be-friends them
chil-dren have   In the Sav-ior's hand;   Fond - ly wins them, Kind - ly brings them
chil-dren sing   Such a Sav-ior's praise? Bow be - fore him, And a - dore him

When they rove;   What a friend the chil-dren have   In the Sav-ior's love.
Ev - 'ry hour;   What a friend the chil-dren have   In the Sav-ior's power.
To his land;   What a friend the chil-dren have   In the Sav-ior's hand.
For his grace;   Should not all the chil-dren sing   Such a Sav-ior's praise?

No. 61. We are Little, yet We Know.

Mrs. S. A. Gates.   E. B. Smith.

1. We are lit - tle, yet we know That the Savior died for us; We can love him here be-
2. We are small, but we can read How he blessed the children dear, Brought to him o'er hill and
3. We are lit - tle, yet we know Jesus loves us just the same, Thus our hearts with love should
4. We are small, but we can love Parents, teachers, true and kind; When we reach our home a-

Chorus.

low, We can try to serve him thus. Lit-tle children, will you hear, While the
mead, In the morn, or heat of day. Lit-tle children, etc.
glow, While we praise his ho - ly name. Lit-tle children, etc.
bove, Love more per-fect we shall find. Lit-tle children, etc.

Sav - ior calls to - day? He is coming ver - y near, He can hear whate'er you say.

No. 62. Little Hands.

J. E. H.   J. E. Hall.

1. Lit - tle hands to work   for Je - sus, Lit - tle hearts to love him, too;
2. Lit - tle eyes to see   for Je - sus, Lit - tle ears to hear the truth,
3. Lit - tle fin - gers point   to Je - sus, Lit - tle throats to sing his praise,

Lit - tle feet to run   for Je - sus; As he'd have us, let us do.
Lit - tle tongues to talk   of Je - sus; Let us serve him in our youth.
Lit - tle souls to give   to Je - sus; Thus we'd serve him all our days.

Little Hands—Concluded.

Chorus.

Je - sus loves the lit - tle chil-dren, Loves to have them do his will.

We would love as lit - tle chil-dren, Pre - cious Je - sus, love us still.

No. 63. There is a Song.

E. E STARKEY.

T. MARTIN TOWNE.

Third Prize Words.

1. There is a song—the grand-est song The chil - dren ev - er sing,
2. There is a name—the dear - est name To mor - tals ev - er known—
3. There is a thought—the sweet-est thought That ev - er chil-dren blest;
4. There is a place— a glorious place, Which he to us hath given,

Caught from the lips of heaven's throng When earth received her King.
'Tis that of Je - sus, he who came For sin-ners to a - tone.
The Sav - ior said, "For - bid them not," And took them to his breast.
Where we may see our Sav - ior's face, That ho - ly place is heaven.

Chorus.

Glo - ry! glo - ry! Be to God in heaven, Glo - ry! glo - ry! For a Savior given.

No. 64. Infant Class Hymn.

E. B. S.   E. B. SMITH.

1. We are lit-tle chil - dren,   But God's ho - ly word   Says "For - bid them
2. When our sins be - set   us,   He will help af - ford,   If we ask for
3. In our dai - ly du - ties,   As we walk a - broad,   We can do good
4. If we live for Je - sus,   Sure is our re - ward,   For no one can

Refrain.

not" from com-ing, Com-ing to the Lord.   Com-ing.   com-ing,
guid-ance, pray-ing, Pray-ing to the Lord.   Pray-ing,   pray-ing,
ser - vice working, Working for the Lord.   Working,   working,
per - ish, trust-ing, Trusting in the Lord.   Trusting,   trust-ing,

Com-ing to the Lord,   Com-ing,   com-ing,   Com-ing to the Lord.
Pray-ing to the Lord,   Pray-ing,   pray-ing,   Pray-ing to the Lord.
Working for the Lord,   Working,   working,   Working for the Lord.
Trusting in the Lord,   Trusting,   trust-ing,   Trusting in the Lord.

No. 65. Bless Us To-Day.

Rev. A. B. EMMONS. From the "International Lesson Hymnal" for 1879, by per.   A. J. ABBEY.

1. Suf - fer the children to come un - to me, Were the pre-cious words Je-sus said;
2. Suf - fer the children to come un - to me, Hear the Sav - ior call - ing so kind;
3. Still he is say-ing, Oh, come un - to me, We'll ac-cept his call and o - bey:

So   we as thy children would come unto thee, Oh, place thy dear hand on each head.
Oh, where but to Je - sus shall sin-ful ones flee, Or where such true happiness find?
With hearts of con-tri-tion we come un - to thee, Oh, bless us, dear Sav-ior, we pray.

Bless Us To-Day—Concluded.

Chorus.

Glad - ly we come, we come un - to thee, Bless us, dear Sav - ior, we pray;

Bless us to-day, Take sin a-way, Bless us, dear Sav - ior, we pray.

No. 66. All for Jesus.

Mrs. Henry L. Chase.   Carrie A. Varney.

1. My two lit-tle hands are for what? With fin-gers so skill-ful and neat,
2. My two lit-tle eyes are for what? To see where the work lies to do;
3. My two lit-tle feet are for what? To run on his er-rands with speed;
4. My two lit-tle ears are for what? To hear what my Sav - ior may say;
5. My one lit-tle tongue is for what? To speak of his praise and his love;
6. My one lit-tle heart is for what? To give to my Sav - ior to - day;

To work for my Sav - ior so dear, On what-ev - er task I may meet.
Our eyes are all made just for that, Whether haz - el, black, or bright blue.
To walk in the nar-row, right path, And help me to each lov-ing deed.
Just lis - ten and hear his kind voice—He says, "Come and serve me to - day."
To call all my friends un - to him, And lead them to meet him a - bove.
To love him, my ver - y best Friend, To tell me the words I shall pray.

Chorus.

All for Je - sus, all for Je - sus, All for bless - ed, bless - ed Je - sus.

No. 67. Little Rain Drops.

Della W. Norton.

J. F. Kinsey.

Moderato.

1. Lit - tle raindrops fill the fountains, Lit-tle birds sing in the trees, Lit-tle sand grains
2. Lit - tle ones can tell the sto - ry Of the blessed Lord who came From his Father's
3. They can learn to sing the praises Of the God who made them all, Who in lov-ing

make the mountains, Little hives are filled with bees; All the lit-tle things are useful,
home in glo-ry, To redeem a world from shame. They can learn to love the Savior,
kindness rais-es Ev - en sparrows if they fall. They can pray, and he will give them

And the children must be, too; There is always work made ready For the lit - tle
Gen-tle answers learn to give, Learn to crown with good be-hav-ior Ev-'ry sin-gle
Fresh supplies of dai - ly grace; And at last he will receive them To his heavenly

Chorus.

hands to do, Lit - tle chil-dren, shout ho - san - na! Raise your voic - es,
day they live. Lit - tle chil-dren, etc.
dwell-ing place. Lit - tle chil-dren, etc.

sweet-ly sing, You are safe be-neath the ban-ner Of the Lord, your Christ and King.

No. 68. Children May Come to Jesus.

C. A. F.   C. A. FYKE.

1. Lit-tle chil-dren, have you heard How the Sav-ior in his word, Says to
2. Lit-tle chil-dren, you may come To the Sav-ior, there is room In his
3. Lit-tle chil-dren, don't de-lay Till the Sav-ior turns a-way, And you're

all his children, "Fol-low me?" How he gave this blest command, When he
lov-ing arms for you to go; He will fold you to his breast, Where there's
left out in the des-ert cold, But ac-cept of Je-sus now, And be-

heard the thoughtless men, "Let the lit-tle ones come un-to me'
joy and peace and rest, And a bless-ing on your head be-stow.
fore his throne you'll bow, When he takes you to his heaven-ly fold.

Chorus.

Let them come un-to me, And for-bid them not, said he;

Let them come un-to me, And for-bid them not, said he, said he;

Let them come un-to me, Let the lit-tle ones come un-to me

Let them come un-to me,

No. 69. Happy in Jesus.

From the "International Lesson Hymnal" for 1879, by per.

A. T. G.
Joyously.

A. T Goram.

1. I am hap - py, oh, so hap - py, pre-cious Sav - ior, in thy love,
2. I am hap - py, oh, so hap - py, for I know that thou art mine,
3. I am hap - py, oh, so hap - py, and my heart is light and free

I could sing from morn till e - ven like the bless - ed saints a - bove.
And thy Spir - it - wit - ness whis - pers that I am a child of thine,
As the bon - nie birds a - bove me warb-ling joy - ous mel - o - dy;

I could tell of thy sweet mer - cy thro' the bright, bright, sun - ny day,
And an heir to life and glo - ry in the death - less sum - mer-land,
I will sing of thee, my Sav - ior, bless thee with my fee - ble breath,

And in joy and ad - o - ra - tion pass the bliss - ful hours a - way.
Where with saints and shin - ing an - gels in my white robes I shall stand.
Till my eyes are closed to life - light and my earth-songs hushed in death.

Refrain.

I am hap - py, oh, so hap - py, I am hap - py, oh, so hap - py,

I am hap - py, yes, I'm hap - py, pre-cious Sav - ior, in thy love.

No. 70. Marching to the Temple.

N. A. C. From the "International Lesson Hymnal" for 1879, by per. N. A. CLAPP.

1. We are lit-tle pil-grims, Hap-py on our way, Traveling on the
2. We are lit-tle sol-diers, Fight-ing for the Lord, Gird-ed with his
3. We are lit-tle Christians, Sing-ing on our way, Work-ing in God's

road that Leads to end-less day; Walk-ing in the path where
ar-mor, Trust-ing in his word; Fight-ing in the field where
vine-yard, Toil-ing day by day; Lead-ing in the path where

An-gels' feet have trod, March-ing to the tem-ple, The tem-ple of God.
An-gels' feet have trod, March-ing to the tem-ple, The tem-ple of God.
An-gels' feet have trod, Oth-ers to the tem-ple, The tem-ple of God.

Chorus.

March-ing to the tem-ple, March-ing to the tem-ple, March-ing to the

tem-ple, The tem-ple of God, Lift-ing high our ban-ner, The

ban-ner of our Lord, March-ing to the tem-ple, The tem-ple of God.

No. 71. Lesson Hymns.

Fourth Quarter's Lessons, 1892.

Old Tune—"Jesus loves me, this I know," (E flat).

MARGARETTE W. SNODGRASS.   E. B. SMITH.

Les. 1. Jesus Christ to-day doth call Ev - ery child, how - e - ver small: Lis - ten, chil-dren! Answer true: "What wilt thou have me to do?"

Chorus.

Sing, Christ of glo - ry! Christ, King of glo - ry! Far tell the sto - ry, How Je - sus came to save.

LESSON TWO.

Life is such a little way,
It may end 'most any day;
Then as heavenward you go,
Do some good each day below.

LESSON THREE.

Never let a thought of pride
Under fairest clothing hide;
All are precious in God's sight,
Rich and poor, and black and white.

LESSON FOUR.

Jesus came to save us all,
Wise or weak, or great or small;
Ask him to forgive your sin:
Come, and he will take you in.

LESSON FIVE.

Little children, up and do!
There is work for all of you:
Speak your words of love so dear,
Give the needy help and cheer.

LESSON SIX.

God is watching here and there,
Every child is in his care:
Though in danger dark as night,
You are safe as in the light.

LESSON SEVEN.

This is what he asks of you—
Such a little child—to do:
Be a Christ-child, kind and sweet,
In your home and in the street.

LESSON EIGHT.

Not to one, or two, or three,
Came the message, glad and free;
Every one may welcome find
In his love so great and kind.

LESSON NINE.

Let your words and deeds be bright,
Pure and clear as blessed light;
Even little lives may be
Lights that all around may see.

LESSON TEN.

Little children, firmly stand,
Doing still your Lord's command;
What though wicked men may chide!
We will stand at Jesus' side.

LESSON ELEVEN

Hearts of love, all warm and true,
This is what God wants of you;
Not an empty outward show,
But a love with steady glow.

LESSON TWELVE.

Are you missionaries true?
Tell what Jesus' love can do;
Send his Word to lands afar,
Where the heathen children are.

LESSON THIRTEEN.

Sing the angel-song again:
"Peace on earth, good will to men."
Sing it in your heart and life,
Till it quiets every strife.

No. 72. Lesson Hymns.

First Quarter's Lessons, 1893.

Old Tune—"Little drops of water," (C).

MARGARETTE W. SNODGRASS. T. MARTIN TOWNE.

Les.1.Come.ye lit - tle chil - dren, Rich-est treasure bring, Pur - est love and ser - vice Un - to God, your King.

Chorus.

See, the light is shin-ing From the God of truth, Shin-ing for the a - ged, Shin-ing for the youth.

LESSON TWO.

Praise him, ever praise him,
  He is good and great:
Praise him in the temple,
  And where'er you wait.

LESSON THREE.

God is up in heaven,
  Yet on earth below:
He is with his people
  Wheresoe'er they go.

LESSON FOUR.

Come, oh, come to Jesus!
  He will make you pure;
Keep you now and ever,
  Happy, glad and sure.

LESSON FIVE.

"Not by might nor power,"
  Thus the Lord has said:
Only by his Spirit
  May his child be led.

LESSON SIX.

Hasten, little children,
  To the house of prayer;
Come with praise and gladness,
  God will bless you there.

LESSON SEVEN.

In the time of trouble,
  In the time of grief,
God will be your helper,
  He will send relief.

LESSON EIGHT.

Even little children
  Need to watch and pray,
In their busy working,
  In their happy play.

LESSON NINE.

Love the holy Bible,
  Study it with care:
God has sent a message,
  You will find it there.

LESSON TEN.

Blessed is the Sabbath,
  Day of sweetest rest!
Keep it pure and holy,
  Give to God your best.

LESSON ELEVEN.

Help the poor and needy
  Near you every day:
Shower words of gladness
  All about your way.

LESSON TWELVE

Listen, little children,
  God's commands obey:
From the wine that sparkles
  Turn your lips away.

LESSON THIRTEEN.

Like a lamp to guide us
  In the darkest night,
Shines the precious Bible,
  Every word a light.

GENERAL INDEX.

TITLE OF PIECES IN HEAVY FACE; FIRST LINE IN ROMAN.

	No.		No.		No.
A LITTLE CHILD,	23	**JESUS, BLESSED JESUS,**	33	NOW to thee our voices	33
A little child I know I am,	23	Jesus, bless us,	37		
All for Jesus,	66	Jesus died on Calvary,	20		
A star shone in the heavens,	38	**Jesus, gentle Savior,**	46	OH, how I love Jesus,	19
		Jesus, gentle Savior,	30		
BIRDS ARE SINGING,	12	Jesus, gentle shepherd,	37	Our Father's care,	16
Blessing the little ones,	41				
Bless us to-day,	65	Jesus, hold my little hand,	4		
		Jesus is the friend of children,	29		
CHILDREN, hear the Savior	7	Jesus I will follow,	4	Pilgrim band,	47
Children may come to Jesus,	68	Jesus' little flock,	11	**Praises,**	12
Christ at Bethlehem,	51	Jesus loves the little children,	49	Praise the Lord,	17
Christmas carol,	38	Jesus loves the little ones,	28		
		Jesus loves us,	14	**SABBATH DAY,**	3
		Jesus make me lowly,	32	Savior, bless me.	45
DEAR and loving Savior,	6			Savior bless me, let me be,	45
Dear Jesus, we bring thee	9	Jesus sees me every day,	43	**Savior lead us all the way,**	31
		Jesus watches o'er me,	43	Say, No,	8
		Jesus we thy flock would be,	11	Sing, O sing,	54
GENTLE JESUS,	42			Sing to the king,	54
Gentle Savior,	30			Something for you,	39
Gifts for Jesus,	9	**Let the children sing,**	56	Something to do,	27
		Let the children's voices blend,	3	**Suffer the children to come to me,**	53
God clothes the lilies of the	16	**Let the little children sing,**	20	Suffer the children to come	65
God makes my life a little light	25	Let them come to me,	7		
God sees the little sparrow	59	**Little children,**	49		
Guide us, loving Savior,	6	**Little rain drops,**	67	**TELL ME ALL ABOUT JESUS,**	52
		Little children, have you heard	68	The care of Jesus,	40
HAPPY CHILD,	32	Little children, love each other	55	The children's friend,	60
Happy hearts,	68	Little children, praise the Lord	17	The morning star,	44
Happy in Jesus,	69	**Little Christian workers,**	13	**There is a song,**	63
Hear our cry,	15	Little feet,	36	There is a song, the grandest	63
He loves me too,	69	Little feet are weary,	36	There is something on earth	27
Home above,	5	**Little hands,**	62	There's a beautiful home,	5
How blest and happy must	50	Little hands to work for Jesus	62	The sweetest words I have	53
How I love Jesus,	19	Little hearts from thee may	31	This is the sweetest story,	48
How Jesus feels,	10	**Little lambs,**	18	**Two little hands,**	35
How sweetly Christ, the	44	Little lambs of Christ are we	18		
		Little light,	26		
I AM happy, O so happy,	69	**Little ones,**	28	**WE are happy little pilgr,**	2
I am little,	21	Little ones, little ones,	39	We are little children,	64
I am little but I love	21	**Little pilgrims,**	2	**We are little gleaners,**	67
If on some pleasant Sabbath	8	Little raindrops fill the foun	67	We are little pilgrims,	70
I know the blessed Savior	56	**Little words of kindness,**	22	**We are little yet we know,**	61
I love to think of Jesus,	41			We have a good and gentle Lord,	1
I'm a little pilgrim,	24	Long ago on Christmas night	51	**We'll not give up the Bible,**	26
I'm glad the golden sunlight	58	**Love each other,**	55	We're a little pilgrim band,	47
		Lovingly the blessed Savior,	40	**What a friend the children have,**	60
Infant class hymn,	64	Loving Savior, well we know	15	When little children let sinful	10
I rather would tell them to Jesus,	34			Who will come and take a	13
I've two little hands to work	35	**MARCHING TO THE TEMPLE,**	70		
		My two little hands are	66		

INDEX OF PIECES IN THIS BOOK,

Which may be sung to Old Tunes, together with the numbers of the Old Tunes, as given in COMPREHENSIVE INDEX. Also, of other Tunes in the book to which they may be sung, as given in METER INDEX.

Nos. of Tunes in this Book.	Nos. of old Tunes as given in Comprehensive Index.	Letters of Meter, as given in Meter Index.	Nos. of Tunes in this Book.	Nos. of old Tunes as given in Comprehensive Index	Letters of Meter, as given in Meter Index.
1	4	B	41	2, 6	E
2	5	C	43	7	D
6	2, 8, 9	A	44	4	B
9	9	F	45	3, 5	D
11	3, 5, 7	D	46	2, 8, 9	A
14	3 5	C	50	4	B
16	4	B	51	57	D
18	57	D	55	3, 5	C
21	3, 5, 7	D	56	2, 6	E
22	2, 8, 9	A	58	2, 6	E
25	4	B	59	4	B
26	2	C	61	3, 5, 7	D
28	2, 9	A	62	1, 3, 5	C
30	2, 8, 9	A	67	3, 5	C
31	5	C	71	9	F
32	8		73	6	
36	8, 6		74	1, 3, 5	
37	2, 8, 9		75	3, 5, 9	D
40	3, 5		76	6	

COMPREHENSIVE INDEX

OF FAMILIAR TUNES TO WHICH THE HYMNS OF THIS BOOK MAY BE SUNG.

NOTE.—In some cases it will be necessary to slur one or more notes, and occasionally to sing two eighth notes in place of one quarter, or two quarters in place of one half.

EXPLANATIONS OF TERMS USED.—o. c., *omit chorus;* o. c. m., *omit chorus of music; r. c., repeat chorus;* d. v., *sing double verse;* r. l. l., *repeat last line.*

No. 1.—JEWELS. (Gospel Songs.) (Key E.) 31, 62, 74.

No. 2.—I WANT TO BE AN ANGEL. (Key D.) 6 (o. c.), 22, 26 (o.c.), 28, 30, 37, 41 (o. c.), 46, 56 (o. c.), 58.

No. 3.—ALWAYS CHEERFUL (Royal Diadem.) (Key E.) 2, 11, 14, 21, 31, 40, 45, 55 (r. c.), 61, 62, 67, 74, 75.

No. 4.—HOLD THE FORT (Gospel Songs.) (Key B♭.) 1, 16 (r. c.), 25, 44, 50, 59.

No. 5.—WHAT A FRIEND WE HAVE IN JESUS (Gospel Songs.) (Key F.) 2, 11, 14, 18, 21, 31, 40, 45, 51, 55 (r. c.), 61, 62, 67 (o. c.), 74, 75.

No. 6.—BECAUSE HE LOVES ME SO. (Key F.) 26 (o. c.), 41 (o. c.), 56 (o. c.), 58, 73 (repeat), 76.

No. 7.—JESUS LOVES ME, THIS I KNOW (Key E♭.) 11 (o.c.), 18 (o. c.), 21 (o.c.), 43, 51 (o. c.), 61 (o. c.)

No. 8.—LITTLE DROPS OF WATER. (Key C.) 6 (o. c.), 22, 30, 32 (o. c.), 36 (o.c.), 37 (o. c.), 46 (o. c.)

No. 9.—YIELD NOT TO TEMPTATION. (Gospel Hymns.) (Key B♭.) 6, 9 (o. c. m.), 22 (o. c. m.), 28 (o. c. m.), 30 (o. c. m.), 36 (d. v., o. c. m.), 37 (o. c. m.), 46 (o. c. m.), 71 (o. c. m.), 75.

INDEX OF SIMILAR METERS.

NOTE.—In this Index the numbers of tunes are arranged in classes in respect to meter. Generally the words of any given number may be sung to the music of any other number in the same class. In some cases, however, it will be necessary to sing two syllables to one note; at other times to slur or tie them together; sometimes to omit chorus, or sing double verse. The chorister should look carefully to this, and try pieces before attempting to sing with the school.

CLASS A.—6 (o. c.), 22, 28, 30, 46.

CLASS B.—1, 16 (o. c. m.), 25 (o. c. m.), 44, 50, 59.

CLASS C.—2, 14 (o. c.), 31 (o. c.), 55 (o. c.), 62, 67.

CLASS D.—11, 18, 21, 43, 45, 51, 61, 75.

CLASS E.—41, 56, 58 (o. c.)

CLASS F.—9, 71 (d. v.)

www.ingramcontent.com/pod-product-compliance
Lightning Source LLC
Chambersburg PA
CBHW021537270326
41930CB00008B/1294